Scholarships: Quick and Easy

By Devon Coombs

Edited by Scott Prewitt

Ordering Information:

Quantity sales. Special discounts are available on quantity purchases by corporations, associations, and others. For details, contact the author at the address above.

I dedicate this book to the love of my life, Michelle. I'll never be able to thank you enough for your loving support.

About the Author

    Devon Coombs graduated Magna Cum Laude from California State University, Northridge's Accountancy and Business Honors programs. While at CSUN, he earned the University Scholarship, the Thomas C. Bloch Achievement Scholarship, the Noski Family Scholarship, the Torchbearer Award, and the Outstanding Graduating Senior Award among many other awards and scholarships. He also was president of both CSUN's Business Honors Association and the Leaders in Alliance Organization. He is also the chief producer of content for Business Core Tutoring.

    Devon is extremely active in the community. He established a mentor program between CSUN and Granada Hills Charter High School, through which high-performing college students mentor high school students. He also created over 100 educational tutoring videos for CSUN. Devon regularly mentors college students and has helped many earn scholarships. He also tutors and advises students in matters regarding financial aid, scholarships, accounting, and finance.

<u>Acknowledgments</u>

This book was the culmination of many peoples' hard work. I could not have done it without my editor, Scott Prewitt, my God-family (especially Cynthia Cummins), all of my scholarship donors, particularly the Noski Family, and Michelle Yu, the love of my life. Also, thank you to all the professors who wrote me letters of recommendations, which helped me earn all of my scholarships.

How to Use This Book

To begin this book, I am going to tell you what this book is not. This book is not a list of scholarships. Scholarships are constantly changing and it would be impractical to write a book that listed each one at the date of publishing. It is not a guarantee that you will win thousands of dollars with little to no work. It takes hard work, initiative, and dedication to win scholarships.

Now let us talk about what this book is. This book does provide clear and concise guidelines to finding and applying for scholarships. It will inform you on practical ways to lower your college debt through financial aid. This book tells you how to get scholarships and where to look for them.

I followed each of the steps in my book to obtain my seven scholarships. I strongly believe that if you follow my advice, you will drastically improve your odds of getting scholarships. I have also talked to many scholarship committees about my advice, and everyone I have talked to assures me that my book is an essential guide to understanding the scholarship process.

I encourage you to first read this book all the way through before you apply for scholarships. After you read it through once, you can reference the "Takeaways" at the end of each chapter to refresh your memory. I also recommend using this book as a reference during any step of the scholarship process.

You can find free supplementary YouTube videos to each chapter at: *https://www.youtube.com/channel/UCbUTIo_011OiffB_FF U-ptQ*. I encourage you to watch the videos after you read the book, or while you read it.

Thank you again for purchasing my book. I wish there was a book like this that I could have read before I attended college. I hope you find it enjoyable and useful.

Contents

Introduction

Attending college is time-consuming and difficult. For many people with limited financial resources it may seem impossible. Fortunately, there are many ways to minimize the cost of college, and perhaps the best method is to obtain scholarships. I know you may have heard this many times before, but I can personally attest that scholarships are the best way to finance your college education. In order to explain why I am so confident in that assertion, I would like to first tell you a little bit about myself.

As I write this book, I am a graduating senior at California State University, Northridge (CSUN). I will be earning two degrees; one in Accountancy with an option in Professional Accountancy, and the other in Business Honors. Most importantly, I will be graduating with NO DEBT.

On the surface, that may not seem like a significant accomplishment. You might think I received money from my parents – I didn't. You might guess that I have a college fund –another no. You might assume I have a wonderfully lucrative job – nope. I am graduating with no debt, and that is significant because I support myself financially.

I searched desperately for ways to pay for college without taking on debt. I worked multiple jobs, tutored students, and minimized my spending. However, the best and most lucrative support for my college education came from scholarships. While at CSUN, I won seven scholarships, which totaled in over $40,000 of aid. I was awarded so many scholarships that the financial aid department had to cut me off – they could not legally give me more money to attend school. If I had put a greater emphasis on obtaining scholarships at the beginning of my educational career, I believe I would not have needed to work a single day while I was in school. With that time, I could have graduated faster, focused more on my studies, and more completely enjoyed my time in college.

If you follow the steps in my book closely and work diligently toward obtaining scholarships, I am confident that you too can graduate with little to no college debt.

Finding Scholarships

There are multitudes of areas in which you can find scholarships – a simple online search can confirm that. However, I would not recommend applying to every scholarship you find online. Instead, contact your university's financial aid department, your professors, and the dean of your college. These people will be much more valuable to your search, as they will know exactly where, when, and how you can apply for the most appropriate scholarships. They can also help write your recommendation letters, advise you on your scholarship applications, and be a resource throughout the entire scholarship process. I once told a friend he should ask his professor for scholarship advice. When my friend got around to asking his professor for help, the professor helped him apply for a $1,000 scholarship that day; the professor turned out to be on the scholarship committee, and awarded the $1,000 to my friend in less than a month. As you can see, these relationships are extremely valuable!

I tried applying for scholarships I found online, through my school, professional organizations, and ones my friends recommended – I have tried just about any place you can imagine searching for scholarships. I never received any from online scholarship search engines; all of the scholarships I received were through my school or professional organizations.

WARNING - Many websites try to steal your personal information, and pose as "scholarship finders." Do not enter your social security number, or any personal identification information online, if it is not a school or government website.

Takeaways

- Utilize your school resources for scholarships.
- Do not look for random scholarships online – only use legitimate resources (your school or professional organizations).

- Ask your professors, deans, and university's financial aid & scholarship department about scholarships for which you can apply.
- Professors will lead you to legitimate scholarships – they might even help you get the awards!

FAFSA Application

Although this book is about scholarships, I highly recommend that you submit the Free Application for Federal Student Aid (FAFSA) at https://fafsa.ed.gov/. I have met many students from a variety of backgrounds and tax brackets who have benefited from filing the FAFSA. The federal government gives a significant amount of free money to college students who demonstrate financial need.

To apply, you will need:

1. Your tax information, or your parents', depending on your dependency status.
2. An official individual identification number, such as your social security number or driver's license.
3. All of your own personal information, as well as your parents, depending on your dependency status.

The FAFSA is an extremely valuable resource. Not everyone uses it, but everyone definitely should. It is not likely to cover all of your college expenses, but it certainly helps! In addition, the financial aid departments at most colleges and universities will help you fill out the FAFSA.

Lastly, make sure you fill out the FAFSA as close to October 1 as possible (it used to be January 1, but they changed the period for the 2017-2018 academic year). Please note that the FAFSA may change this date again in the future, so please reference its official website for application deadlines. Federal aid is limited and distributed on a first-come, first-serve basis. The sooner you apply, the more likely you are to receive the maximum federal financial aid assistance.

Takeaways

- Use the FAFSA Website: *https://fafsa.ed.gov/*

- **DO NOT USE ANY OTHER WEBSITE CLAIMING TO BE FAFSA, IT COULD BE A SCAM!**
- Apply for the FAFSA as close to as October 1 as possible.
- Even if you may not be eligible for FAFSA support, still sign up – you may be surprised and get free money.
- Many university financial aid departments require that you first apply for FAFSA before you apply for scholarships.

Applying for Scholarships – Timeliness

One of the greatest areas of struggle for college students is their ability to finish work in a timely manner. Scholarships usually have submission deadlines for your application, letters of recommendation, résumé, and essays. If you miss the date, you are ineligible for the scholarship. This is a harsh reality – to benefit from the scholarship, you must do your work ahead of time and make the scholarship's deadline.

When I transferred to CSUN from Pierce College, I was determined to get scholarships. When I contacted CSUN's Financial Aid Department, a representative directed me to a website that listed all of CSUN's scholarships. However, before I could gain access to the scholarship database, I had to turn in a personal statement, letters of recommendation, and two essays. This was a lot of work, so I procrastinated. I told myself, "There is no way that I am going to miss these scholarships. I'll finish the application after summer." I did finish the application after summer, as I said I would. Unfortunately, all of the scholarship dates had expired the week prior. Had I finished the scholarship process just one week earlier, I could have potentially doubled my amount of scholarship earnings. That was a particularly unforgiving lesson, but an important one nonetheless. Always turn in your applications weeks before the deadline, so you do not make the mistake that I did.

Takeaways

- Timeliness when applying for scholarships is essential - if you miss an application deadline, you will **not** be considered for the scholarship.
- It is easy to put off work, but **DO NOT** fall into the same trap I did. Prepare your letters of recommendation and essays as soon as possible.

- I have met many people who could have earned thousands of dollars in scholarships but did not because they **DID NOT MEET THE DEADLINE!**
- Timeliness can make or break your scholarship applications.

Applying for Scholarships – Letters of Recommendation

Professors' Letters of Recommendation (Includes University Faculty and Deans)

Letters of recommendation from a professor can be among the most authoritative types of recommendations. A letter of recommendation from a professor shows that you are a good, intelligent student, and took the time to develop a relationship with an academic professional (all of which are aspects that scholarship committees find impressive). Also, the professor that writes you your recommendation may be on the committee for the scholarship you are applying for. Therefore, developing these relationships and asking for recommendations could be instrumental in getting lucrative scholarships.

I find that many students struggle with getting letters of recommendation from their professors. This continues to surprise me, because professors will generally give you a recommendation letter if you:

1. Give the professor at least two weeks to four weeks' notice when requesting a letter of recommendation.
2. Provide the professor with a short autobiography so they can get to know you better.
3. Provide the professor with your résumé or transcript.
4. Ask professors you get along with.
5. Ask professors whose classes you perform well in (A or B grades).

DO NOT BE INTIMIDATED BY PROFESSORS! They are a resource to you; many professors teach because they want a connection with their students. Spend time at your professors' office hours and develop relationships with them.

I would recommend asking four or five professors for

letters of recommendation. It is likely that one or two will be too busy to write you a recommendation, or may write the letters too late. Asking multiple professors will protect you from the risk of getting too few letters. Stop asking professors for letters of recommendation once you have secured three, as you should not need more than three letters for any scholarship (to my knowledge).

Also, a more generic letter will allow you to apply to more scholarships without having to bother your professors multiple times. So, when asking your professors to write your recommendation letters, request that they make them universal. Ask that they write the letter to recommend you for "any and all scholarships," or something along those lines.

Furthermore, request digital copies of all of your letters of recommendation. Many scholarships allow you to submit copies of the originals, which will speed up the application process. In addition, many professors will appreciate that you are not bothering them as much when you are applying for multiple scholarships.

However, some professors may be opposed to this concept, and some scholarships may require that the professor send recommendation letters directly. First and foremost, ALWAYS follow your professor's and the scholarship's instructions over this book's recommendations.

Lastly, thank your professors for their efforts! Writing a good letter of recommendation takes time, so you should foster the relationship with your professor with a thank you note. And, of course, keep the professors up to date with the scholarships they helped you to secure – odds are, they will be appreciative!

Employers and Personal References

Your secondary types of recommendation letters are from employers and volunteer organizations. I strongly recommend getting at least one recommendation letter from your employer, as many scholarships require this.

Recommendation letters from friends and family are your last resort – they will not hold nearly as much authority as one from a professor or an employer. Only get letters of recommendation from friends and family if you have exhausted all of your other resources. Because I am adamantly opposed to getting recommendation letters from friends and family, I will only discuss employer letters in this section. Letters from volunteer organizations follow the same rules as letters from employers.

When asking for a recommendation letter from your employer, follow similar steps to what you would do for a professor. Instead of giving your employer your résumé or transcript, give him or her a short autobiography or a draft letter with points you would like covered in the recommendation. Make sure you request that your employer makes the letter generic and gives you a copy (preferably digital). Also, inform your employer that he or she may be contacted by the scholarship committee to verify his or her existence. Employers generally work quicker than professors do, but I would still recommend giving your employers at least two weeks to finish their recommendation letters.

Takeaways

- Ask at least five people for recommendation letters.
- Obtain a minimum of three recommendation letters.
- There are five sources for recommendation letters:
  1. University faculty (professors, deans, and administrators).
  2. Staff (academic advisors, program coordinators, etc.).
  3. Employers.
  4. Volunteer organizations (churches, nonprofits, etc.).
  5. Friends and family.

- University faculty, employers, and volunteer organizations are the best resources for recommendation letters.
- Letters from friends or family are a last resort.
- Get digital copies of your recommendation letter if possible or permitted.
- Give your recommenders two to four weeks to write your letter (the more time the better).
- Request that your recommendation letters be generic and universal (to apply for all scholarships).
- Give your recommenders a short biography, transcript, and résumé so that they can write more about you.
- Thank your recommenders for their time, and keep them up to date with the scholarships they helped you secure!

Applying for Scholarships – Essays and Personal Statements

The essay portions of scholarship applications can be extremely intimidating. As I mentioned in the introduction, I missed an entire year's worth of scholarships because I procrastinated on my essays. Do not let the essays intimidate you – there are plenty of resources to help you get through them (this book being one). If you follow my steps, you will be just fine.

1. Start Writing Rough Drafts Early

The most time consuming aspect of scholarship applications is the essay portion. Start writing your essays as early as possible. Almost every scholarship requires a personal statement. Usually, the statement must be at least 250 words, and rarely will it be longer than 500 words. I recommend writing a rough personal statement and catering it to whatever essay you are required to write. I spent a few hours a week for approximately one month writing and revising my essays. Having a large time frame to write your essays will give you more time to work with editors, which will reduce your chance of making mistakes.

2. Get Help Editing

Do not be afraid to ask your friends and family to help you edit your essay. You should write the core substance of your essay — **DO NOT PLAGIARIZE** — but have people you trust review your essay. When I wrote my personal statement, I repeated this process until it was excellent.. The editing process can be time-consuming, but it is essential to a well-written essay.

Also, make sure that your editors are people you can trust and who make you comfortable. Personal statements and essays can get very, well, personal. My editing process was a lot more comfortable because my English-major friends commented on my essays openly. It was a long process — I would write an essay, bring it to my friends, they would review it, then I would edit it and bring it back to them. Choose people who know your life story and who you will not feel judged by.

Also, there are a multitude of campus resources you can use to help you edit your essays. Ask the financial aid department at your campus if there is anyone who can help you edit your essay. You can also ask if your campus has a writing lab, tutoring lab, or learning resource center. Each of these programs is generally under-utilized by students, so I highly encourage you to take advantage of them!

3. Make It Personal

Most scholarship committees want to know your story — why you are pursuing an education, why you are interested in your field, what hardships you have overcome, and so on. The more you can connect with your readers, the more likely you are to get a scholarship. So make your scholarship essays authentic, personal, and real. Be direct and avoid flowery language, but try to convey emotion in your writing. Most committee members who read scholarship essays appreciate concise, powerful essays, as they have to read hundreds of other essays. Honesty is refreshing. Whatever your position is in life, the reader will appreciate if you speak from your heart.

4. Save Your Essays

I have applied to over 30 scholarships in the last two years, each requiring one to three essays. You might think this was a daunting amount of work, but it really was not! Many scholarship essay topics overlap. All you have to do is use an old essay and alter it slightly for the new scholarship. I have submitted over 90 essays for scholarship applications, and most were derived from just four original essays! It is perfectly legitimate to use your old essays and repurpose them for new essay topics.

5. Remember – Writing Essays Makes Financial Sense

I spent close to 50 hours writing and editing my scholarship essays. However, I received well over $40,000 in scholarships. $40,000 divided by 50 hours is $800 per hour. You will find no better-paid job in college than scholarship writing— if you know of one, send me the details immediately!

Takeaways

- Essay writing is time consuming – start writing your essays as soon as possible!
- Most "Personal Statement" essays are very similar – I recommend you start working on your personal statement as soon as possible.
- **DO NOT PLAGIARIZE.**
- Get help editing – use school resources, friends that are good at editing, or parents to help guide and refine your essay writing.
- Be genuine and authentic. Everyone has a story to tell, so tell yours. People appreciate honesty, and will be more likely to help you on your journey if you are willing to share your story.
- Save your essays and reuse them. Many scholarships have similar essay guidelines, so you do not always have to write new essays.
- Essay writing and scholarship applications could potentially be the most lucrative job you have in early life. I made over $800 per hour for my essay writing and application process, and I know many who have had similar luck (10 hours of writing and applying for $8000 in scholarships).

Review and Submit Your Applications

You have searched for all of your relevant scholarships, obtained your letters of recommendation, and written your essays: now what?

1. Review Your Applications

- Check your applications for accuracy, spelling, and grammar.
- Ensure that you have met all of the requirements and submitted all of the paperwork.

2. Review, Submit, and Organize Your Recommendation Letters

- Use the most relevant recommendation letters for the appropriate scholarships.
- Let your recommenders know that they may be contacted by whoever is granting the scholarship.
- Store your recommendation letters electronically. If they are physical copies, scan them and save them on your computer.
- Organize your recommendation letters for future reference.

3. Review, Submit, and Organize Your Essays

- Check your essays for grammar, spelling, and content errors.
- Make sure your essays meet the word requirements (scholarship committees normally disregard any scholarship essay that is over the word limit).
- Submit your essay in the scholarship's required format, while making sure your desired format remains consistent (sometimes paragraph structures can be different in online applications).

- Save your essays on your computer and organize them for future use and reference.

4. Relax and Wait for Results

- Great job, you have applied for multiple scholarships! If you followed all of the steps in this book, I strongly believe that you will have significant success obtaining scholarships.
- Do not be discouraged if you do not get the first scholarship you apply for. There are plenty of scholarships, and being rejected from one should not bother you. Even though I was awarded well over $40,000 in scholarships, I was rejected from many scholarships as well. Wait it out!
- Now that you have all of your resources in order, you can apply for scholarships every semester with the same materials. You now have an amazing source of revenue that will help you graduate debt-free, and with minimal effort.

Takeaways

- Spend a lot of time reviewing your essays and applications. Spelling and grammar errors could get your application removed from consideration. I would normally spend 2 hours reviewing my application and essay for every 1 hour I spent writing, and I recommend that you do the same.
- Organize and submit your recommendation letters.
- Wait and relax. You have done your hard work; now just enjoy yourself while you wait for your responses.
- If you do not win scholarships your first round, do not become discouraged. You can't win them all, and scholarship committees often reward persistence.

What Scholarship Committees are Looking For

I have been fortunate enough to meet and interview many scholarship committee members. In this section, I am going to tell you exactly what they are looking for when selecting candidates. I am also going to elaborate on the average scholarship screening process. Understanding the committees' screening and selection process will give you a huge advantage over other applicants. It is a two-step process – (1) screening and (2) selection. Be sure to understand this process well! Also, know that financial aid departments make the screening and selection process as objective as possible.

The Process: Screening

A scholarship committee must first screen all the applicants for proper qualifications. The committee will read each application and make sure the applicant meets all of the scholarship's requirements: GPA, class standing, number of recommendations, number of essays, financial aid qualifications, due dates, or anything else that could limit the applicant pool. This is not a qualitative process; the committee is just making sure that you meet the scholarship's basic requirements. They discard applications that do not meet the appropriate requirements, and keep the ones that do for further deliberation (the qualitative aspect of the process).

Now that you know that committees screen for a scholarship's basic requirements, make sure you actually meet those requirements! I have heard from many committee members that they kick out multiple applications during this process because many applicants do not meet the mandatory criteria. Even worse, many applicants leave out letters of recommendation, essays, or miss due dates. Only apply for scholarships you are qualified for, and finish all of their requirements on time!

The Process: Selection

Now the scholarship will have a pool of screened applicants. Each member of the committee will read each application in detail and give it a score on a weighted score sheet.

Normally, a weighted score sheet will look something like this:

Category	Score (1-5) (5 is high)
1. Student Leadership	
2. Community Involvement	
3. Writing Skills	
4. Applicant's Passion for Field of Study	
5. Overcoming Adversity	
Total	

Figure 1

The aspects that are scored (the 'Category' column) change based on the donor's and committee's preference. Each committee member will score each applicant according to his or her ability to demonstrate these aspects. The committee members will then pool their scores, and find the top applicants. The highest scoring applicants win the scholarships. If there is a tie between top applicants and the committee has limited awards, it will debate over who should receive the scholarship.

You can use this knowledge to your advantage.

Understanding how a scholarship is weighted – and knowing what traits the donor values most – is essential to winning. Read the scholarship's description carefully and try to address each point of the scholarship in your essays and application. Let us look at some of the ways you can score high in the categories listed in Figure 1 above.

1. Student Leadership

Many scholarships require students to have participation with student organizations. I strongly encourage every student to apply for leadership roles in at least one student organization. If you are still in high school, I highly recommend Academic Decathlon, DECA and/or Debate teams. If you are unable to obtain a student-leadership role, at least become active in a student organization. Scholarship committees highly value leadership, and joining a student organization will give you an edge over your competition.

2. Community Involvement

Whether you are applying for a job, a school, or a scholarship, committees will always look favorably upon community involvement — meaning volunteer service. Become active in groups and organizations that interest you as soon as possible. Personally, I actively mentor students in addition to volunteering at my church. For the latter, I help with sound and media as well as aiding with the church's accounting. I genuinely enjoy volunteering. Why? Because I choose to volunteer in roles that I already enjoy. I am an advocate for mentoring and education; therefore, I predominately volunteer for these causes. Volunteer for an organization in a role that you enjoy, and you will be ahead of your competition.

Try to avoid volunteering for causes that you have no interest in, as they will be difficult to write about enthusiastically in your scholarship essays. Authenticity is extremely important. Committees can tell if you genuinely cared about a cause, or if you used it as a space "filler." Always follow your passions, even when you are volunteering. Passion for a cause will help you differentiate yourself from the competition. In addition, volunteer positions are a great addition to your résumé.

3. *Writing Skills*

Scholarship committees will judge an applicant's writing skills based off his or her essays and personal statement. Generally, scholarship committees heavily weigh writing skills, which is why it is essential that you perfect your scholarship essays.

It was mentioned earlier, but it is worth saying again: If you believe your writing skills are weak or could use some work, I highly advise you seek help from either an editor, a tutor, or a friend you fully trust to look over your application. It is not an exaggeration to say your future may depend on it.

4. *Applicant's Passion for Field of Study*

Passion is persuasive. One of the scholarships I applied for had a huge level of involvement from the donor, who actually hand-selected the scholarship's recipient based on the passion the winning applicant displayed for his or her field of study. I have heard of many similar selection processes for scholarships. Therefore, you must convey your passion through your writing. Specifically, try to write about why you are passionate for your field of study, or the fields of study you are considering pursuing.

5. *Overcoming Adversity*

Unfortunately, most people have faced some kind of adversity in life, be it the loss of a loved one, financial hardship, discrimination, isolation, a family issue, or so on. Scholarship committees appreciate honesty with these issues, and want to know about the obstacles you have faced in life and how you have overcome them. Your past troubles may help the scholarship committee or donors connect with you. I encourage you to be honest in your essays about the difficulties you have had in your life. Sharing your story can benefit you greatly, and might make your future a bit easier.

In an effort to lead by example, I have included my personal statement at the end of this book. This statement tells the story of how I overcame adversity in my own life, and it may help you get started on your own story. To you, sharing your personal story might seem scary. However, to those reading it (whether they are fellow students or scholarship committee members), a story about overcoming the odds in the face of overwhelming adversity can be a powerful inspiration. Try to be that inspiration, for your own sake and for the sake of those who may benefit from your words of hope.

Takeaways

- There are two steps to a scholarship committee's process – (1) screening and (2) selection.
- Understanding how the scholarship committee screens and selects its winners is instrumental to you winning multiple scholarships.
- Make sure you understand the requirements of the scholarship.
- Tailor your essays and experience to the scholarship.
- Develop the following target-areas for scholarships:
  1. Student Leadership.
  2. Community Involvement.
  3. Writing Skills.
  4. Passion for your Field of Study.
  5. Overcoming Adversity.
- Remember each scholarship has different criteria. Your understanding of each scholarship's criteria is what will set you apart.
- Your school's scholarship office may be able to help you determine a specific scholarship's criterion.

Different Types of Scholarships

Below, I will quickly mention three different types of scholarships. Understanding how different types of scholarships are judged will give you an advantage during the application process.

Professional Scholarships

Professional organizations often give scholarships. State-based Certified Public Accountant organizations (such as the CalCPA in California) offer aspiring accountants yearly scholarships. Ask your college's financial aid department about the various professional organizations that offer scholarships for students in your major or discipline. These professional scholarships rest heavily upon applicants' community involvement and passion for the field. Emphasize your commitment to these principles in your applications for professional scholarships.

Merit-Based Scholarships

Some scholarships are based purely off merit — grade point average (GPA), volunteer work, writing skills, and leadership. Merit-based scholarship committees are looking for the most qualified student that meets their criteria.

GPA:

Merit-based scholarships generally require that you maintain a minimum Grade Point Average, the lowest of which is normally a 3.0. You will qualify for most scholarships by earning a GPA higher than 3.5. Approximately 30% of the scholarships that I received required me to have above a 3.5 GPA, and about 70% of them required me to have above a 3.0.

Volunteer Work and Leadership Positions:

Volunteer work is also essential for Merit-Based Scholarships. Merit-based scholarship committees are searching for outstanding volunteer work that exceeds the minimum requirements established by the committee. One of the most prestigious awards I won at CSUN was the "Outstanding Graduating Senior Award." It required me to have a cumulative GPA of above 3.5, to make significant contributions to CSUN and the community, all while displaying exceptional personal achievement (http://www.csun.edu/studentaffairs/ogsa). The volunteer work that I did for my community and school included running the CSUN Business Honors Association as President for one year, creating a mentor program between the Business Honors Association and a local high school, and creating over 100 tutoring videos related to coursework that my fellow students were struggling with.

So, what can you learn from my efforts? GET INVOLVED IN YOUR SCHOOL AS SOON AS POSSIBLE. Try to get leadership positions in clubs and organizations that you care about – if you can't get a leadership position, make your own club or program. Also, look for ways improve your school and community; once you find the issues, take efforts to solve them. I promise you, a little effort in these areas can go a very long way. Also, merit-based scholarships look great on résumés and are a wonderful conversation starter. Although I am only mentioning why it is important to do volunteer work to obtain scholarships, you will experience innumerable other benefits from such works.

Writing Skills:

Many merit-based scholarships require lengthy essays beyond your personal statement. Please refer to my general advice regarding scholarship essays for this section. Just remember, the competition for merit-based scholarships will be more difficult than other scholarships, so make sure you have no spelling errors or grammar mistakes in your essays!

Need-Based Scholarships

Need-based scholarships sound like what they are: scholarships determined by your financial need. Similar to the FAFSA, need-based scholarship committees will determine if you demonstrate financial need through you and your parents' or guardians' income. If your total income is below a certain threshold, you may be eligible for these awards. I encourage you to apply for each and every need-based scholarship that you are eligible for – if you are not sure if you are eligible, discuss the details with your scholarship department. I have met many people who originally thought they made too much money to get need-based scholarships, but discovered they were eligible after a minimal amount of research.

Combination Scholarships

Many scholarships include a combination of the before-mentioned requirements. Some may be partially merit-based and need-based, while others may just be purely need-based. Do not be intimidated by these requirements. Try to find which scholarships you are most eligible for and apply to them. Understanding how these scholarships are selected will help you focus on the scholarships you are more likely to win.

Takeaways

- The three main types of scholarships are:
    1. Professional
    2. Merit-Based
    3. Need-Based
- Find professional organizations in fields that interest you or involve your major, and apply to their scholarships.
- For merit-based scholarships, try to keep your GPA above a 3.0, or preferably above a 3.5. More scholarship opportunities will be available to you with this GPA threshold.

- Become active in your school and community as soon as possible – despite innumerable other benefits, you will improve your leadership experience and become eligible for many more scholarships.
- Research your eligibility for need-based scholarships. Even if you make money you still may meet the requirements for some of these scholarships.
- Many scholarships have a combination of the above-mentioned requirements.
- Use your knowledge of the different types of scholarships to focus your efforts on ones that you will have the most success with earning.

After You Have Won Your Scholarships

Congratulations, you have won some scholarships! Each scholarship comes with prestige (they look great on résumés), money, a great sense of pride and accomplishment (and occasionally even a nice banquet). You might think it is time to sit back, relax, and enjoy the debt-free, full-ride scholarship life. Sorry to disappoint you, but you still have a few things left to do before that gets to happen.

1) Thank You Letters

Most financial aid departments require you to write a thank you letter to the donor who awarded you the scholarship. Even if they do not have this requirement, I recommend that you write a thank you letter regardless. Your donor could be a valuable resource to you in the future. Taking the time to write a simple letter of appreciation could lead to you getting a mentor for life. Furthermore, write it as soon as you are awarded the scholarship. The donor and the financial-aid staff will appreciate your promptness. At the very least, your donor deserves a letter for all that money they just gave you!

2) Banquets and Donor Meetings

For some of the more prestigious scholarships, you may get a chance to attend a banquet, meet your donors, or meet distinguished faculty such as the university's president or your college's dean. It is imperative that you dress up for these events, show up on time, and express your gratitude to your sponsors and donors. I have met some incredible people at these banquets. Some of those people have written me letters of recommendation, some have offered me valuable career advice, some were willing to mentor me, and some did all of these. Such banquets might seem intimidating, unnecessary, or even boring, but these dinners are amazing opportunities to meet successful (and charitable) people who can help you throughout your life.

3) Ongoing Requirements

Some scholarships require you to fulfill certain ongoing requirements (GPA, community service, etc.). Make sure you actively fulfill each requirement. One of the scholarships I was rewarded required me to fulfill four hours of specific community service a semester, maintain a 3.5 GPA, and pursue other aspects of academia (either research or a faculty mentor). I was extremely busy during the first semester that I was awarded this scholarship (with volunteer work, ironically), and did not meet my community service requirement. I had to scramble over winter break to fulfill my requirement, and my scholarship was nearly suspended. Do not let that happen to you! The next semester, I finished all of my scholarships' requirements in the first week. This gave me a lot less stress and was appreciated by the financial aid staff.

Takeaways

- Write thank you to your donors as soon as you have been awarded your scholarships.
- Dress up for all of your awards banquets.
- Show up on time for all of your awards banquets.
- Remember: You could be meeting a future mentor at one of these awards banquets!
- Accomplish all of your ongoing requirements as soon as possible, or your awards may be rescinded or suspended!

__Conclusion__

Thank you for reading my short book on scholarships. If you followed these steps, I am confident that you have greatly increased your odds of obtaining thousands of dollars in scholarships. I truly hope the advice I have given here will help you minimize your college debt, graduate with better grades, and live a better life, all by working smarter rather than harder.

To supplement this book, I have made a YouTube video of each chapter on the "Business Core Tutoring" channel: _https://www.youtube.com/channel/UCbUTIo_011OiffB_FF_ _U-ptQ_. You can also search for "Business Core Tutoring" in Google to find the channel. I encourage you to follow along in the book, and in the videos, to obtain the most help. Also, please feel free to write to me with your scholarship success stories — I would love to publish them.

Lastly, if you feel like there is something I can do to improve my content, I would be more than happy to do so if at all possible. I am also eager to hear any suggestions you may have about other topics you would like me to address, whether in print or video. Feel free to write me any time at businesscoretutoring@gmail.com. Thank you for reading my book. I wish you the best of luck with your education, scholarships, and the promising careers that follow!

Example Personal Statement

"Your mother passed away last night."

My stepfather's cold tone was surreal. He was the one who always threatened suicide; she was not supposed to die. The man was stuck raising two teenagers that he had not the least bit of interest in, and despised the fact that he had to do it on his own. He did not want to live; how could he be a father?

I fell to the wayside. This man had no inclination to nurture me, unlike my half-brother, as I was not of his blood. He never wanted to adopt me. Any attempt I made to connect with him was in vain. He showed no interest in my ambitions, and when I turned 18 he told me I would have to find my own accommodations. Abruptly, I went from having an overprotective, loving mother to fending for myself.

My mother always taught me that if I worked hard and strived to be a good person I could achieve anything. She was attending community college when she passed away, and she wanted nothing more than for me to be a college graduate one day. In an attempt to respect my mother's wishes, I worked diligently at an assortment of odd jobs while attending community college part-time. I saved money and rented out an office, in which I built a recording studio. I hired employees and created a business that focused on recording bands, developing promotional strategies, and releasing albums. Maintaining my enterprise while attending college and supporting myself proved to be excessively demanding and I lost the business. However, I continued working and attending school while living out of my car so I could pay off my debts. I worked as a server, bartender, tutor, busser, promoter, personal assistant, and salesperson- anything that had the potential to give me the stability I needed to attend school. With every free moment, I found enjoyment in volunteer work; I walked dogs for local animal shelters, and helped the administrators for the Revlon Run and the

Challenged Athletes Foundation.

My biggest frustration was that I desperately wished to attend college full-time, but my life was so unpredictable that I could not; I had no support system. I watched my well-off peers graduate and become more secure, while I was forced to work full-time and at multiple jobs just to survive.

After all of these hardships, a few people learned of my past and became my mentors. I had the opportunity to work as a CPA's interning auditor over summer, where I discovered my passion for public accounting. In just four months, I went from being a basic intern to being entrusted with the task of completing the audit of a million-dollar non-profit with minimal supervision. I decided to pursue accounting and was fortunate enough to find a job serving at a local café that accommodated my school schedule. In addition, I found a woman with an incredibly kind heart who let me live in a spare bedroom inexpensively, which gave me the security I needed to continue my education.

After many difficult years, I am finally finished with community college and have received my associate degree in business administration. I have been accepted to CSUN's pre-accountancy program, and I have a clear goal: my bachelor's degree in accounting. Most importantly, I have a way to accomplish my mother's dream for me, and I desperately wish to make that dream a reality, for her and for myself. One day I hope to pursue my Master's of Science in Taxation and a CPA license. Despite being at the top of my class, I still struggle with balancing 25 to 40 hours of work a week, tutoring, and going to school full-time. I live on a shoestring budget. I know if I was able to work less and focus on college more exclusively, I would be able to excel scholastically as well as contribute more to my community.

Example Scholarship Essay (Less than 400 Words)

My peers, my past, and my ceaseless ambition motivate me to excel in my majors. I am earning a double major in accounting and business administration, with an option in business honors. These majors challenge me to learn as much as possible about finance, accounting, and business. My mother raised me in poverty, and I never met my father. My mother passed away when I was 15, and my disinterested guardian made me fend for myself when I turned 18. Ever since then, I have been independent. My mother always wanted a better life for me; she dreamed of the day that I would be a college graduate. Her postmortem wish motivates me to excel in my majors. Furthermore, I desire to raise a family outside of poverty, as well as help my community.

As a potential University Scholar, I have a multitude of goals. I am a member of the institute of managerial accountants, and I plan to pass their rigorous two-part certification exam before spring of 2016. I will also be an auditing intern at Deloitte, the largest public accounting firm in the world, this upcoming summer; I will actively help CSUN students with Deloitte's challenging recruiting process. Additionally, I will volunteer as a lower division business tutor for four hours a week. I will also continue to be active in Beta Alpha Psi, and other community efforts. Moreover, I am making free tutoring videos to assist students with challenging accounting, math, and finance concepts. If the system I make for the videos proves successful, I will do my best to implement it throughout all of CSUN's colleges. I am also the Vice President of Finance for the Business Honors Association, and I will maintain leadership roles in student organizations until I graduate.

My experiences at CSUN will assist me greatly over the next 10 years. CSUN's accounting and business honors programs have created a foundation of ethical, technical, and practical knowledge for me; these skills will help me earn my certification in public accounting, excel in my career, and lead my community. CSUN has also distilled a desire in me to constantly challenge myself, which will lead me to continuously educate myself throughout my life. In addition, I will continue to play a leadership role in my church, my community, my work, and my future alma mater (CSUN).

Made in the USA
Middletown, DE
05 February 2018